No, No, NO!

Published by
MAGINATION PRESS
An Educational Publishing Foundation Book
American Psychological Association
750 First Street, NE
Washington, DC 20002

For more information about our books, including a complete catalog, please write to us,
call 1-800-374-2721, or visit our website at www.apa.org/pubs/magination.

Printed by Phoenix Color Corporation, Hagerstown, MD

Library of Congress Cataloging-in-Publication Data

Callier, Marie-Isabelle.
[Non et non pas question. English]
No, no, no! / by Marie-Isabelle Callier ; illustrated by Annick Masson.
pages cm
"Originally published in French as Non et non pas question by Mijade Publications (Belgium)."
ISBN 978-1-4338-1311-5 (hardcover : alk. paper)—ISBN 978-1-4338-1312-2 (pbk. : alk. paper)
1. Interpersonal conflict in children—Juvenile literature.
I. Masson, Annick, date, illustrator. II. Title.
BF723.I645C3513 2013
155.4'182—dc23   2012043775

First printing February 2013

10 9 8 7 6 5 4 3 2 1

by Marie-Isabelle Callier

illustrated by Annick Masson

No, No, No, No!

MAGINATION PRESS • WASHINGTON, DC
American Psychological Association

Jeanne is a little girl
who loves to play, sing, and dance.
When Jeanne played in the park,
she was as happy as can be!

But afterward, when Mom asked her to change into clean clothes,
Jeanne's mood changed. All she could say was,
"No, no, NO!"

In fact, whenever Mom asked her to do anything, Jeanne said,
"No, no, NO!"

Mom asked her why. Who was this little dragon who always said no?
Jeanne couldn't explain.

Jeanne left her toys all over the house.
"Jeanne! Time to pick up your toys and turn off the TV.
Please wash your hands. We're about to eat dinner,"
said Jeanne's mom.

Again Jeanne replied,
"No, no, NO!"

One day, Mom lost her patience
and raised her voice.
"Jeanne, I've had enough! Stop
saying no all the time!"

But Jeanne screamed even louder,

"NO, NO, and NO! No way!
You're not my mom anymore!
I want another mom!
I want Sophie's mom. SHE is nice!"

Mom was upset, but said nothing.
The next day, Jeanne went to a sleepover at Sophie's.
Mom packed her little dragon's overnight bag.

When they got to Sophie's house,
Mom gave Jeanne a quick goodbye kiss.
As soon as Jeanne saw her friend, she ran off.

The girls played all afternoon,
and had lots of fun.

Jeanne and Sophie could have played forever.

But before dinner, they had to put everything away.

Jeanne didn't dare say no, but she started to pout.

When it was time to wash up before dinner, Jeanne still wanted to play,
but she followed Sophie without a grumble.

Then it was dinner time.
The soup didn't taste the same as her mom's.
Jeanne felt her little dragon coming back…and she said "NO!"

Sophie's mom wrinkled her brow
and frowned a little.
So Jeanne finished her soup quietly.

That evening, Jeanne's mom went to a movie all by herself.

When it was time to go to bed,
Jeanne felt a little squeeze around her heart.

Sophie's mom read stories really well,
but who was going to give Jeanne her nighttime hug?
Jeanne felt like crying.

Luckily for Jeanne, her mom had thought of everything!
Jeanne found a special note from Mom beside her stuffed animal.

Sophie's mom read it to her and very sweetly wished Jeanne and Sophie a good night.

The next morning, as soon as she woke up,
Jeanne looked out for her mom.

When the doorbell rang,
Jeanne ran to the door and threw herself into her mom's arms!
They hugged for a long time.

Jeanne said goodbye to Sophie
and left hand-in-hand with Mom.

On the way home, Mom said
"I'm happy to see you!
Did you have a good time?
Would you like to invite Sophie over on Saturday?"

Jeanne smiled. This time she said, "YES!"

Note to Parents and Other Caregivers

by Elizabeth McCallum, PhD

Defiance in young children is a normal—though often unpleasant—part of child development. As children move from toddlerhood into childhood, they are able to do more for themselves and rely less profoundly on their parents to meet their daily needs. They are now able to accomplish many activities by themselves for which they previously relied on parental assistance. For instance, they can now get dressed on their own, feed themselves, use the bathroom by themselves, and choose their preferred activities independently. Unfortunately, with this increased independence often comes an increase in defiance. Preschoolers often refuse to comply with their parents' requests, or ignore those requests altogether. While this newfound defiance can be extremely frustrating at times, it is important to keep in mind that it is a normal part of childhood. There are steps you can take to reduce your child's defiant behaviors and the stress that is associated with them.

HOW THIS BOOK CAN HELP

In the story, Jeanne refuses to comply with her mother's requests. She replies "No!" when her mother asks her to clean up after herself, turn off the television, and come to dinner. Most parents of preschoolers can identify with this situation. Reading this book to your child can be a fun way to discuss the issue of defiance without speaking specifically about your child's own behavior. By discussing Jeanne's defiant behavior, children may be more likely to engage in conversation about the topic than they would if discussing their own similar behaviors. After reading the book, you may wish to ask your child if he notices any of Jeanne's behaviors that seem similar to his own. This can be a springboard for talking about how you feel when your child says "No!" or ignores your requests. For example, you might say something like, "Jeanne's mom felt frustrated when Jeanne said 'no.' Sometimes I feel frustrated when you say 'no' too."

COPING WITH NORMAL CHILDHOOD DEFIANCE

Preschoolers defy their parents as a way of asserting their independence and testing boundaries. While defiance can be upsetting, remember that it is a normal stage of childhood development, and that it will pass. In the meantime, there are steps you can take to reduce your child's defiance and increase your resources for dealing with it. The following are guidelines for coping with normal childhood defiance.

Set limits and follow through with consequences. Consistency is important for all children. Set clear boundaries and consequences for failing to follow the rules. Your child should know the rules and consequences for breaking these rules. Be consistent in your enforcement of the rules and delivery of consequences. If your child sometimes breaks a rule without receiving a consequence, she will likely continue to break the rule because she knows she may be able to get away with it. Try to avoid rewarding your child's defiance by giving in to her demands.

Use positive reinforcement. Deliver praise or small rewards contingent upon appropriate behavior. If your child brings her plate to the sink after dinner, tell her that you are proud of her for doing so. If she puts on her shoes when you ask her to do so, give her a sticker and thank her for following your request. Particularly with young children, a little bit of positive reinforcement can go a long way towards increasing good behavior.

Encourage independence by allowing your child to make choices. Whenever possible, allow your child to have a say in deciding his activities. Let him choose what shirt to wear to school or what song to listen to in the car. Not only will this reduce his frustration at being constantly told what to do, it will also encourage individuality and help him to identify and refine his interests.

Pick your battles. Some behavior is not worth fighting over. While you probably must insist your daughter wear a certain dress to be the flower girl at your sister's wedding, you may want to allow her to choose her own outfit to wear to the park.

Set realistic expectations for behavior. Try to match your expectations for your child's behavior to his age and skill level. When you ask your child to do something, make sure he knows how to do it. Sometimes, defiance can be a child's way of saying "I don't know what to do." Model the appro-

priate behavior for him and help him to be successful at completing the task.

Put yourself in your child's shoes. Try to consider the situation from your child's perspective. If your child is watching his favorite television show, it may be difficult for him to switch gears and immediately come to the dinner table when you ask him to. Instead of abruptly calling him to dinner, give him a "five-minute warning" before it's time to transition. He may still complain or resist when you insist he comes to the dinner table and that's okay. Be consistent with your rules and expectations and eventually he will learn that defiance will not get him what he wants.

Have a sense of humor. Despite your frustration, try to see the humor in the situation. After all, a mother being "fired" by her four-year-old (as Jeanne's mom is in the story) is pretty funny!

Defiance is normal and is one way that children assert their growing independence. In all likelihood, it is a phase that will pass. However, if your child's defiant behavior persists, or interferes with school or his social life, it may be helpful to seek consultation from a licensed psychologist or psychotherapist.

Elizabeth McCallum, PhD, is an associate professor in the school psychology program at Duquesne University, as well as a Pennsylvania certified school psychologist. She is the author of many scholarly journal articles and book chapters on topics including academic and behavioral interventions for children and adolescents.

ABOUT MAGINATION PRESS

Magination Press is an imprint of the
American Psychological Association,
the largest scientific and professional
organization representing psychologists
in the United States and the largest
association of psychologists worldwide.